Poetikayl Solution
My Character House
Book One

Marcell Anthony Wallace

Instagram: *Poetikayl Solution*

Outline

Dedication

I dedicate this book to the pursuit of truth, morality, love (in the Hebrew concept of 'ahab') and integrity.

Preface

Welcome to *My Character House*. If you will, please leave your shoes at the door. I recall those days when my grandmother used to yell at us "If you don't take those shoes off! Tracking that filth and dirt around the floor I just swept and mopped! Y'all betta' show some respect!". *"Aaah",* as I sigh thinking, "Thanks Manete for those indirect lessons." I often refer to those lessons now which are very much instrumental in my character development.

Therefore, feel free to have a seat and get comfortable. "Would you care for anything to drink? Snack on? Hospitality being key, I have to keep in mind the golden rule in, "treating others how I desire to be treated."

One thing you'll learn about character, when it comes to each person, it differs from personality or the outward appearance and mannerisms. Although we all have unique exterior and interior designs of personality, we all gravitate to the same moral foundations of character.

As you sit in comfort or decide to walk around and read the poetic expressions throughout the halls of my walls. I encourage you to take notes as you flip through each page to **Book One** of *My Character House.*

THE MEANING BEHIND THE COVER

I'm sure you noticed on the front cover the emblematic illustration of the animal carrying the golden house (denoting transparency of my life's experiences through my poems). Below is provided the descriptions of each Hebraic concept.

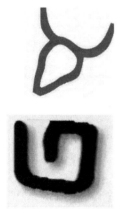

The picture to your top left is the ancient pictograph form of the Hebrew letter, **Aleph,** representing **strength , or leader**

The picture to your bottom left is the ancient pictograph form of the Hebrew letter, **Beth,** representing **house, tent or family**

When combining the letters **Aleph** and **Beth.** It forms the Hebrew word **Abba** or when translated into English, **father.** It can also mean, **the one who brings strength to the house or family.**

Character V Personality

Question

HAVE YOU EVER MET A PERSON WHO

PRESENTED THEMSELVES AS
SOMEONE WHO WAS

INTELLIGENT

FUNNY

WELL-SPOKEN

AND OUT-GOING

BUT LATER ON, WHEN YOU
REALLY GOT TO KNOW THEM
YOU WERE SOMEWHAT ANNOYED
AND DISAPPOINTED

WELLLL

THE REASON I'M HERE IS TO
WELL INFORM YOU, INFORM
YOU WITH INFORMATION THATS
VITAL UNTO

Your Journey

Give you an opportunity to explore,
some of the things
that are important for your growth

One is to show why you felt annoyed and isappointed
like many others.

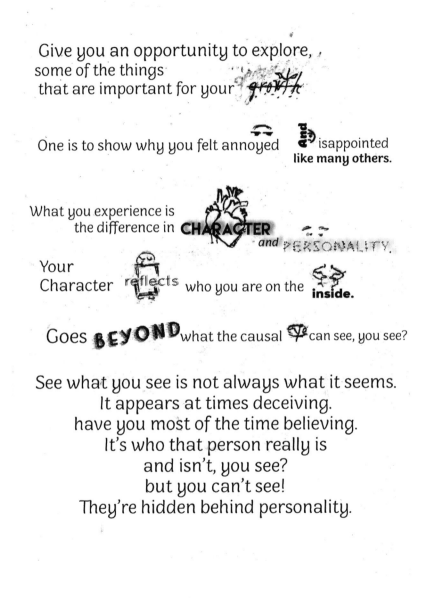

What you experience is
the difference in **CHARACTER** and PERSONALITY.

Your
Character reflects who you are on the **inside.**

Goes **BEYOND** what the causal can see, you see?

See what you see is not always what it seems.
It appears at times deceiving.
have you most of the time believing.
It's who that person really is
and isn't, you see?
but you can't see!
They're hidden behind personality.

Only by Observation of that person's pattern of behavior

When they are *faced with a moral choice.*

will they tuck tail or stand straight?

that's the basis of weighing options

your

Stopping *and* **Thinking** before you choose to pursue.

See our every thought, action, decision

derives from our inner.

It is the means by which we distinguish between

Right and **wrong**

The foundation of our **backbones**

In short

all I'm saying is

No one is totally devoid of the positive.

It's normal that we tend to gravitate

more towards those with compatible personalities.

What I like, you could like.

Dislike. Prefer.

WE ALL DIFFER!

Just be careful and remember,

If you want to later avoid those disappointments,

lost friendships and divorces

it's best first to get to know them.

Many times we get confused with that fine line

between character and personality.

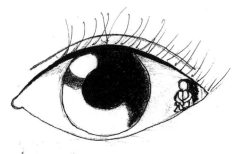

Living
In
The
Eyes
Of
Others

I DESIRE TO BE A PUPIL IN THE MOST HIGH'S EYES... INSTEAD

I'm living
   in the eyes
of others.

   The standards
  they set
   within these walls.

  less concern with how they view things
the optic NERVE of them!

Did they notice my insecurities? Probably not.
Guess I'll always be the blind spot in the subconscious.

Influences

picks at my self-consciousness,

led me to buy new clothes

to cover my obscurities.

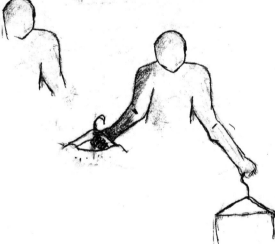

The amount of time I spent
looking through their lens.
The self-criticism I put in!
    Afraid to do what I know to be right
    Trying to be pleasant in their sight
       And then,

they close their lens.
   those are my fears
      flowing from their lachrymals!

I apologize!
if I ever was an irritation
standing in your projection.
The red in your sclera
symbolize the internal pain
I endured and I'm tired

Swimming through a temporary fluid struggling
to gain your acceptance

I'm lost!

especially when there's no light
coming through your cornea.

In essence,

I made you the beholder of beauty of my imperfections.

The peer-pressure in your stare,

I was captured by the wink of conformity in the retina!

deceived by the personality of your iris

In the mirror of your eyes
that added insult to injuries.
It shows me how ugly I am,
how handsome I could be,
how depressed I look,
or
it could neglect,

a reflection, reflecting what's skin deep

and that..

I should focus more on the things that make

me unique like my love, loyalty and respect.

Instead only on situations

and or physical characteristics.

I.. Have No.. Control Over.

Think of every person as miniature worlds

We revolve around our natural resources.
Abundance in our supplies

Created for the purpose to be inherited
to be protected by the micro-kind
man,commanded from our skin
to be like lotion beneficial to prevent
our ground from cracking

because we know
with the pressure from the universe
weighing heavily on our shoulders
could be a burden on our heart-core
ready to hyper-compress in oil,rich.

but not for our own self-interest.
Yes we be self-sufficient.
But sharing! we the world!

21

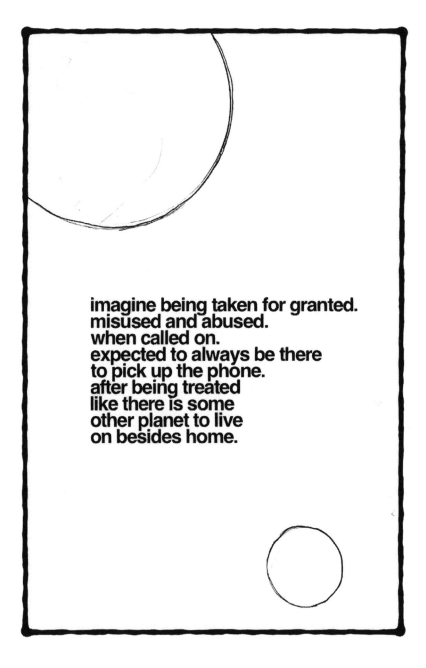

imagine being taken for granted.
misused and abused.
when called on.
expected to always be there
to pick up the phone.
after being treated
like there is some
other planet to live
on besides home.

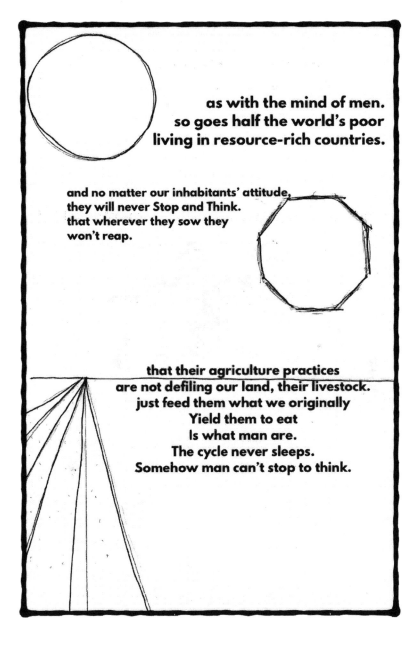

as with the mind of men.
so goes half the world's poor
living in resource-rich countries.

and no matter our inhabitants' attitude,
they will never Stop and Think.
that wherever they sow they
won't reap.

that their agriculture practices
are not defiling our land, their livestock.
just feed them what we originally
Yield them to eat
Is what man are.
The cycle never sleeps.
Somehow man can't stop to think.

that their radioactive PPCPs*
is not changing the gender of its species in the ocean
how deep!
will they continue to drill!
to know that our oil is basically
being fought over by brothers!
if they don't care for each other!
what makes you think they'll care about us!!
got us bathing in a dilute solution of antibiotics.
when less than 1% of our water is drinkable.

*(Pharmaceuticals, Personal Care Products)

24

after waiting too long
to finally go green,
they turned our trees
into greed.
man industrialized whatever
they could get their hands on,
including the skies.
if only they had held
onto that ancient truth
instead of the genetically
altered.

MANKIND THINK!
THOSE ARE CAUSED MICROBES IN
OUR ATMOSPHERE.
WARMING AND WEAKENING OUR
OZONE LAYER.
DESTROYING ALL THE LIFE THAT'S THERE.
THE LIFE COMMANDED TO FORM
ALL LIFE.
MOST MAN HAVE LOST THEIR ABILITY
TO USE SIMILITUDE.
TO MAKE A CLEAR DISTINCTION
BETWEEN RIGHT AND WRONG.

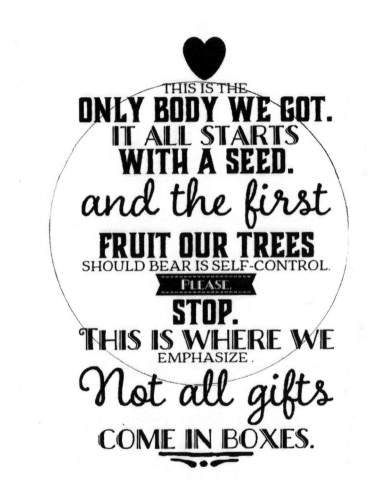

THIS IS THE
ONLY BODY WE GOT.
IT ALL STARTS
WITH A SEED.
and the first
FRUIT OUR TREES
SHOULD BEAR IS SELF-CONTROL.
PLEASE,
STOP.
THIS IS WHERE WE
EMPHASIZE.
Not all gifts
COME IN BOXES.

Offer to lace up in someone else's shoes and walk the extra mile to show, they too have a sense of belonging.

In a world,

that doesn't ask permission, it takes!

Like the inquisition took religious freedom

and burnt it at the stake like,

the KKK had so much hate boiled down,

it was so hard for them to show their face like,

The Jewish settlements,

justify stealing Palestinian's land in claims

it is "god given rights"

So,

Instead of a month for a particular cause,

race or person's history,

It should be a lifetime,

of mental ethnic cleansing

of learned ignorance.

Your own wisdom.

Covert racism.

Prideful attitudes.

Desensitize abnormal values leads to

Superior thinking,

gossiping and bickering.

In these Institutes,

they teach more segregation than they do tolerance

Its the reason hatred,

discrimination,

prejudice,

racism,

generalization and stereotyping exist!

So how long will we sit misjudging

until numbness begets in our maxims?

before awakening at the slam of the gavel to realize?

not just education academic-wise was key.

Yes, we need to learn to write and read but

take heed to what's sinking beneath our feet tho

If respect was taught like wars are fought

we would fault ourselves.

On corner, selves, they sell themselves until they're short.

"Don't tell" the code is what they're taught or else

When self-respect is lost,

The brain is starved.

leave food for thought,

but the thought of food

Tear friends apart.

that love now false.

the sky is Braille,

For minds are dark.

divide then conquer

Comes from the heart.

They build jail cells

to pardon their part.

See Love is respect.

Since war is waged,

respect is far.

the world is mistaught

Too comfortable in its spot.

Its either we coexist or non existence

because in the end we have to.

So take careful consideration

for that person next to you.

Just for a moment,

offer to wear their shoes

and walk that extra mile to see,

how long it took for them to get there.

And when you arrive

then you'll finally begin

to appreciate them for being here.

I don't know why I believe this

if man were created blind..

Possibly we could better SEE

how much we NEED each other.

Because what's so hard with daily common courtesy?

Resurrecting chivalry with kind words!?

Avoiding physical insults and speaking violence verbally?

Practicing moral decency?

Finding worth in everything

including each and every human being?

Every individual is unique and has potential to fulfill his means

Accept more of our humanity.

Just One Drop of blood under the microscope to see.

We are nothing more than Adam's and Eve's

held together by a covalent bonding - miniature molecules.

So why can't we imagine being group together like atoms,

sharing our electrons with our positive charges,

becoming oxygen

for the next generation to breathe!?

With only offering to
lace up in someone
else's shoes,
and walking that
extra mile to show
They too have a sense
of belonging.

"Our lives begin to end. The day we become silent, about the things that matter."

That was Him. a man many believed in. He wasn't.

HIP HOP

"A hip hop, a hippie to the hippie to the hip hip hop, you dont stop a rockin"

that program! Which was about pimping.

and to the bang bang boogie, say up jumps the boogie, to the rhythm of the boogie.."

How is this! Going to teach our children Responsibility

Because in the midst of all this dancing
A child is suffering. A parent is struggling.
because Abba is missing.
Conditioned
that
These are the breaks
Face it.
It's funny but I'm not laughing
That's the breaks that's the breaks"

Domestic violence,
is higher among mothers abusing kids.
Most crimes committed by our sons and
daughters who are fatherless.
but
That's the breaks that's the breaks"
over 1 million teen pregnancies every year
That's the breaks that's the breaks"

and among our young people
most STDs are prevalent.
and our only solution to them:
just use a con-dumb how we gotten.
look how far that its gotten!
and by the way it's gotten,
they have us right where they want us,
self-enslaved!
Physically and physiologically to dem shackles.
And the cry for freedom
never been so bigger than hip hop
And you don't stop. what you can stop. but you choose not.

Murder
In fact, call it *abortion*
no, call it *Choice*
Pride,
Greed,
Beauty,
euphemise it and call it anything except murder.
Yet we are taught to think and say "we are free."
But these are some of the things that hold us captive.

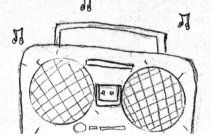

if we, cannot lead ourselves,
then who are our children going to follow?
It's too much fashion
and not enough positive role models.

So

Oh where Oh where have our fathers gone
Oh where Oh where could they beee-

came a culture where childhood is perpetuated.
Unable to mature.
physically grown in a child-state conscious.
Incapable of managing our own lives.

"but i still won't grow up, I'm a grow old kid,
swear i should be locked up for the stupid ish that i did."

Incapable of growing in our own minds.
Got Brendas raising babies.
Not yet ready for the world
make choices uneducated.
a lack in educating,
with all this education.

Dear Mommas,
You are Coretta Scott without the King
a headless queen
and it seems,
you are way too 5 star chick
to find your true means.
Because real stars do not seek to glorify themselves
but rather let the whole universe shine.
they are round like the sun.
Helping to provide energy,
food spiritual and physical
so that our daughters and sons
can expand through time -
Fathers.
It doesn't take Ed OG to be one to your child.
He doesn't need to add another snare kick
to a dead beat
produced by a dead beat
Ghost written by an illegitimate son
so you can glorify your life story.
Because ever since you marched right,
left on your son's first steps,
he's been ever searching his soul looking for you!
that dividing wall separating.
profiting off this segregation
In HER household the title father is discriminating
Not enough for a civil rights move.

He needs you!!
to tell him that its nothing wrong when a man cries.
That you don't have to be perceived as hard to get by.
He needs you to teach him about manhood.
That you don't need to be hood
to think outside of your hood.
Confined in a perpetual state
of moving beyond the hood.
you are a voice!
as much as you are stumbling block.
and these squares never been so hot.
but how can you
when you are mentally a child yourself.

" brotha, brotha, brotha

there so many of you dying "

On and off record.
There is too much beef to be going green,
Everyone is going green
But C.R.E.A.M,
doesn't make the world go round as love do.
Your son's legacy
is predestine because he follows your footsteps.

So here's a revolution,
let's start by raising our family institutions.
Overthrow that prideful government within ourselves.
March back home.
because a house divided against itself will not stand.
All our children need are sit-ins,
10 times out of 10, for us to listen,
Nonviolently demonstrating our position.
So stop with the protesting at your mate's flaws.
We wasn't put on this earth to be at competition.
I have a dream
but it's going to take some empathy.
some responsibility.
A combined effort from you and me.

It seems like
nobody wants to
bear the
responsibility.
Our ability to
respond
seem a little
irritable.
when it comes to
being accountable
for another human being.

That wasn't
My King

Who Am I? pt.1

Out of 3, mama's boys, I'm the middle child.
Marcell Anthony Wallace is the name
my Manete and Mama gave me.
♪♪ *BEANIE!* ♪♪ Wallace is the name that she gave me.
♪♪ *BEANIE! BEANIE!*♪♪
WALLACE is the name that she brand me.
humbled by the sun being 'maid'
is why I carry on the name; my mama's raisin.

But am I..
Am I in a safe sanctum to say, I'm still learning who I am?
I know that I am, of I am, a son of man of Hebrew descent
yet far from hayah Abba Yahweh (I am which exists;
I am who I am; I choose to be righteous)

Im a puzzle with pieces of me everywhere; incomplete.
The head is where I in-compete
the battle more than sciamachy.
fighting the same sins and sanity, in-repeat
Like bruh "didn't learn the first time", in-defeat
Sifting through mental pixels to piece new peace
To be whole and human is integrity.

I must remind me, "it takes time to solve".
Child-adulthood pain dissolved
Words has been my resolve.
Is why I salute sound.
Speaking is how I soul-vent.
Poetry and I are soul-meant.
I am the solution.
Wrapping back around like a bow on a gift
to answering my own rhetorical to who I am
I am.. learning.

Dream

When I grow up
I want to be just what mama dreamed I'll be.
In turn making her dreams a reality.
Becoming better than who she once was.
Because she knew who she once was.
No parent wants their child to go through what they did.
So through blood, sweat, tears and hot sand,
Mama did all she can to make our roads easy.
So "become better son."
As she would always say.
"I got your back son."
"No matter how old you get I'm still yo mama!
And I'll still take care of you."
A mother's love conditional and
unconditional to the condition of critical.
And it's hard to believe mama raised three boys
With twice as much strength
as the males who claim they were men - so called fathers.
Living what mama dreamed
And not her worst nightmare.
A mother shouldn't have to bury her child
Or bail them out
She should rest knowing
They're living her dream.
Of "Please, let my child live to see the next day"
In a world where nothing is guaranteed.
Where they expect a single parent mother
to cope with the stresses of negative influences.
marketed to their impressionable young-minded child daily.
via television, movies, billboard-ads.
Then question the parent's responsibility.
A bunch of hypocrites to those who think they aren't
contributing.

In this world
dreams are considered fantasy.
Standards set low to make it.
Soul sacrificial and dignity if reached.

I know my mother isn't the only parent awake dreaming.
For a college graduate or well-educated,
Successful young man or woman.
Family oriented, their child.
I can see why this is what most parents' dream about.
Because for my child I dream the same.
And it's self evident it's in our children's DNA
to want to please their parents.
To want to fulfill mom or dad's dreams.

You Have Value

You are a walking death bed. Pill-low depressant swallowing addict. Between the sheets unprincipled abomination. Forgetful hearer. Proud bastard. GMO junky. Unhealth freak. Suicidal risk taker. You negative thinker. Pity party. Miserable guest. Unthankful person. Regretful dweller. Verbal murderer. Ignorant story.

A product of this system.

And you wasn't taught value.

So how could you love your neighbor if you don't know how to love yourself?

impossible!

If you're telling someone something else on one hand but on the other hand you're not practicing what you told them..

Please.

Not another excuse.

what ifs'

shouldas', wouldas', or couldas'

No need to go blaming them.

It's a bit irritating.

When I just saw you.

before I spoke with you.

after I reminded you.

TWICE! I had to remind you!

and we agreed on you valuing yourself.

Didn't you just have a heart attack?

Test positive for _?

Almost died in a car accident, drunk?

Released from rehab ?

And yet you go back to the very same ways

that's making your grave.

Were you ever taught value?

You deserve to be self-respected.

44

It just hurts to see someone you do know
mirror someone you don't know
or do know
or could know
or who don't care
or at least show partial concern for his or her life.
And when asked about eating right
Or changing to become a better person.
That selfish unthought out response,
"Im gonna die anyway."
Which shows you wasn't taught value.

To have value means
you take into consideration your worth
as measured in usefulness or importance.

Simply because you exist!
You Have Value

YO BIG POETIC JUSTICE head ahh!

I rather RUN than face my PROBLEMS head ahh!

My washer dryer ALWAYS BROKE can't seem to fix my cycle of behavior.

Thinking with the bottom head LOOKING AHH!

YO BIG illegal LUST head ahh!

OL fire and brimstone waiting if I don't overcome these POOR HABITS head ahh!

OL I CAN'T FORGIVE MY PAST head ahh!

I CAN'T FORGIVE MYSELF for myself head ahh!

OL I prefer to rock unrighteous judgements LOOKING AHH!

YO BIG everybody wrong, sky blue, sky blue except for me head ahh!

OL I can't respect myself long enough to love myself, develop who I am first, I must be in a relationship, can't be alone OL DAMAGED head ahh!

INSECURE head ahh!

MR. I DON'T CARE if my poor choices impoverished others head ahh!

BOARDERLINE NARC head ahh! CODEPENDENT head ahh! SENSITIVE head ahh!

I rather CHOKE and WALK OFF stage before I FINISH A POEM head ahh!

OL I choose people based OFF APPEARANCE head ahh!

ALWAYS ATTRACTING low energies and frequencies BECAUSE THAT'S WHAT I SEEK LOOKING AHH!

OL I can't focus on my craft, ALWAYS DISTRACTED Looking ahh!

always in the Kool-Aid but don't know the flavor head ahh!
I take EVERYTHING PERSONAL. BAD decision making.
THE END OF THE WORLD SEEING AHH!

OL I can never get it right head ahh!
Anger infected kidneys head ahh!
EMOTIONAL TURBULENT HEAD AHH!
I can go on and on head ahh!
When it's all said and done,
I hope to look back and see how far I overcame and enjoy the laugh.
But dang MY BIG YOUNG LOOKING DUMB FULL OF SEMEN HEAD AHH! HAHAHA!

I READ THIS quote:

"A Successful Life
is not
NECESSARILY MEASURED
BY WEALTH or
the accumulation
Of Materialistic things.
True Success
Comes
With Maintaining
A Positive Character.
How you treat yourself
and others
is the
TRUE MEASURE
of success."

It doesn't take an 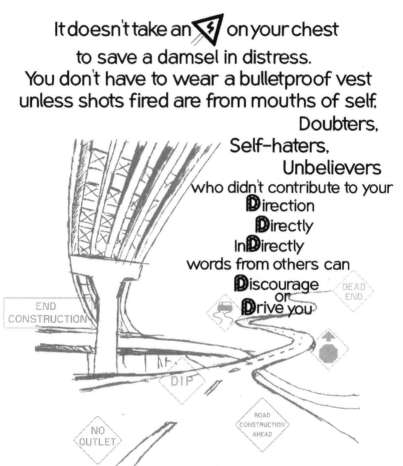 on your chest
to save a damsel in distress.
You don't have to wear a bulletproof vest
unless shots fired are from mouths of self,
Doubters,
Self-haters,
Unbelievers
who didn't contribute to your
Direction
Directly
InDirectly
words from others can
Discourage
or
Drive you

to prove them wrong with your right choices.
And it is ultimately your right choices
that will determine your true success.

what you
consistently do
when others
are not watching you
will determine
your true Character.
Yes!

A cesspool of
OBSTACLES,
SETBACKS.
PITFALLS.
will come in all
SHAPES and **FORMS**
to
SHAPE and **FORM**
the very foundation
your personality
and character
is fathered on.
Lessons
mothered discretion.
Both Parental Advised
the positive
and negative
traits inherent
at conception.

ultimately,
your choices
will beget
a life filled
with regrets
or accolades
from personal
achievements.

Also

Your Influence
has the ability
to infect affect.
Your treatment
is in how you
treat people.
be careful how you
inject your effect.

A moral pandemic
been global.
A Self-quarantine
been warranted.
The reason
the virus
wasn't detected earlier
Because
the sickness is internal.
The cure is also internal.
Antibody your
surroundings.
A healthy immunity
is needed in
survival when
striving for
your purpose.

RELIABLE

HUMBLE

Also

Be a successful leader by self-leadership.
Leading yourself is essential.
People are watching and eager
to emulate your every move.
Know followers are important too.
Followers are what makes a leader true.
you must first be a successful follower
Following the lead,
is how all leaders
became into being.

Also

Be organized not disorientated
Takes into consideration
everything from your time
to your belongings.
In which your most
valuable possession
is your character.

Being disorganized
wastes time and
effort, and cause
frustration and stress.
In the world of a
disorganized person,
everything takes
twice as long,
and goals are
twice as hard to accomplish.

It takes character
to make character.
One immoral act to break character.
It's more than just a word
that consists of nine letters.
Your character defines who you are.

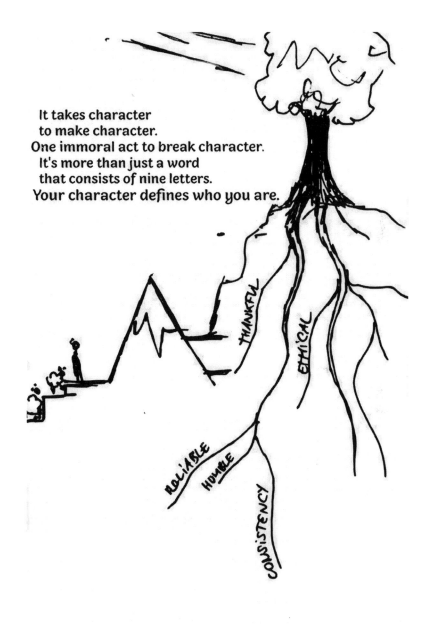

ARE YOU

Consistently
Humble
Accountable
Reliable
Archetype   OR
Courageous
Thankful
Ethical
Responsible

COLD
HEARTED
AMORAL
RULER
ACTING
CALLOUSLY
TOWARDS
EVERYONE'S
RIGHTS

?

To Be Successful

You must dig deep
You ain't deep enough if when you cut
integrity ain't what you bleed.

True Success is based on who we are
NOT who we appear to be.

Regardless of race, color, or creed.
Your skills, energy and talents
can get you where you desire to be,
but your positive moral character
is what you so desperately need
to keep you there, to succeed.

21 Ways On How To Get Out Of The VictimHood

1. When you are under arrest. Do Not Resist. For every thought needs to be placed under subjection.

2. Objection notarizes your emotions while justifies your habitual inactions.

3. Uncomfortably Comply. Call it whatever type profiling. Your mind needed that traffic stop.

4. Face fear. The probable cause is on the grounds of you being too complacent.

5. You know "hands up. don't shoot" was a lie? So please stop perpetuating this lie to yourself. Best keep it one hundred with you before dem boys in blue do.

6. Fake your death. Then miraculous come back to living life but attempt to live it right this time. Don't be too comfortable being a target walking dead.

7. No one on earth or in the heavens is going to save you.

8. If somehow you escape and deadly force is used, don't be bleeding your fear on everything and everyone around you. Stop and think before you make a scene, putting the people in that same guilty by color mindset.

9. Anything you think to say will be used against you in the courts. You have the right to a counselor. If you can't afford a counselor, you will be appointed for someone to account you through this.

10. Even if it's not your fault. You are learning to be responsible. You Are Learning To Be Responsible. YOU ARE LEARNING TO BE RESPONSIBLE.

11. Excuses are the real noose. We hang like familiar fruit. So avoid becoming a nuisance.

12. The crime you circus'd in your mind before it manifested into reality's innocence. Guilty until proven you can be freed from the prison within.

13. I know, it's scary. But what's even scarier is being trapped behind those mental bars days, month, years on end, knowing you could have been accountable. Knowing you could have less wasted and more quality time on self-improving. In other words, if you know you did or didn't do the crime, still snitch on yourself.

14. Blaming history, hereditary, genetics, psychology, socioeconomic, white supremacy, educational institutions, the system, the government, PTSD (Post Traumatic Slavery Disorder) any narrative outside of you.... is a cop out.

15. I know racism and people who choose to accentuate those negative traits within, exist. I ain't "ignant". I'm aware of stop and frisk. But in my Eric Thomas' voice: "It's probably going to be racism 'til the day you die quit crying about it."

16. You wanna know the irony of history. History is the study, of the past . Even Western Philosophy have us cemented. grounded. a well familiar place when apprehended. They have us thinking the past is behind, while the future is front of us. However, how Eastern Hebraic ancestors' thought, the future was always behind;

blind to them. The past was always present; in front, for what we know to avoid. <u>So study history to know what to avoid</u>.

17. If you got knocked down five or ten years ago and I come back and yo butt still on the ground! Don't allow repeated defeat to be your story.

18. The true police brutality is you abusing your mental wealth. Irresponsible with loving yourself. And abandoning your duties and blaming someone else. So you be the authority that commands yourself before you try command others.

19. Hug yourself before you hug the block.

20. Stop thinking the world is out to get you. Stop! The only entity out to kill your goals and dreams is **you**. And if the world kills you for overcoming you. Your legacy should live on.

21. **You Have The Rights** to make the rest of your life the best of your life. **Get Out The VictimHood**.

"Communicate unto the other person that which you would want him to communicate unto you if your positions were reversed."

Aaron Goldman

Cease The Tension

I need to mention among enemies, friends or significants
arise conflicts, disagreements or dissects

a direct result of,
a breakdown communicating effectively.
Rejecting thee,
basic concepts of eye to eye contact.
Body language, facial express
conveys the full meaning of the dialogue.
the two involved.
Putting forth ears heart soul and all
to get the point across.
Each attentive.
Giving respect.
Not waiting to opinion
but waiting to reflect the response,
To show the speaker that you're listening
To show him or her, their deserved worth.
Compassion, putting those first.
And if ya minds are like mine
True peace never brought hurt
And Never Will.
So get interested
interact with some common sense,
it'll most definitely cease tension.

Listen

Communication is more than just talking
over a hot instrumental
You're teaching the youth by your actions
and fractions between your fellow rappers
and miscalculations;
they're jotting down notes
while you're writing out your problems
without solving them.
Intolerance
plus Inconsideration
plus Racism
plus Discrimination
is the **equation** of Hatred.
Subtract the verbal and physical violence
All we need is attention **undivided**
and **R** for the **Remainder**
So **Respect** is required of us.
Don't just give it to get it,
Give it because its the right thing to do.

If you compare communication to a song,
Your tone of voice would be the music
that accompanies the words.
Of course we all love a great beat so
the tone of voice you choose
gives meaning to your words.
As momma always taught:
"It's not what you say but how you say it
and to whom you are saying it to".
That's shows respect to other individuals.

But if someone disrespects you
the easiest thing to do would be to get even.
This is where we **stop, think** and **consider** that

retaliation begets more retaliation.
And that all this back and forth
will only create an atmosphere of added hatred in our
minds.
then with isolation comes
diss track.
on top of
diss track.
on top of
diss track.
until you're one track-mind.
When it only takes one person to stand up
for what won't cause harm to others themselves or the
environment.
It takes two to positively interact.
So become the one to be that sounding board
and **LISTEN.**

There's Words Then There's Actions

All I hear
is spoken sound behind a one-sided mirror
of you sound proof.
Everyday.
What's done in the light is seen from the dark.
I observe
the ninety percent scene you act out
like a early nineteenth hundred silent film
in pantomime HD.
yourself, out of control
when **you think** no one isn't watching
because **you thought**
your words undercover for you.
You felt the strength roll off your tongue into language
opposite from physical activity,
I believe what you were saying.
I was convinced.
A reflective response, my heart was in.
I trusted you were a person of spoken sound.
But only by observing a person's pattern of behavior,
when they are faced with a moral choice
from an overwhelming black room
you can see the transparency of their words
unveil in the saturation of escape.
of them actually believing
what's reflecting back at them from a mirror
they think no one was watching
For the first time
they felt the confidence roll off their tongue,
and got away without touch.
But like a stab in the back
does not literally mean a stab in the back,

63

when words can manifest to do it for us.
And every conversation now
shouldn't be that of a short attention span child.
when the only thing that grabs my attention
is an over exaggerated emphasis of habitual tendencies -
increased volume.
that compose letters are if not the last thing
I'm separating into spaces
trying to comprehend the inconsistency
on why are you saying one thing yet doing another!?
See words
can either show care, concern,
embarrass, frighten or threaten.
Consequently,
words can also show, our character.

It's Vital To Make This Exchange

How else to convey knowledge and information?
I want to tell you what I'm thinking and feeling
that is satisfactorily received.
As we stand on opposite ends of this page
A need for both of us to comprehend to what each one of us
is saying.
So let us work together effectively like
words used, in the correct tone,
as our facial expresses what our bodies are speaking,
in order for us to hear and feel what we are saying,
ya feel me?
Not if you're not hearing I'm what saying.
Of course, it goes both ways.
For this relationship to be successful,
There must be a mouth and all ears and a control of self
as one person must give the information,
The other must be willing and able to take it in,
that's why it's important for us to make this exchange.
Ironically,
the way in which we engage often leads to
misunderstandings.
Either will leave one or both of us standing internally or
externally hurt.
This is how conflicts start.
And relationships and marriages are torn apart.
And words can lead to a family, community, gang or world
war.
That's why this exchange is so vital to our coexistence.
That without this exchange
There is no point in living!

Imagine with me
being joyful, sad, upset or scared
and having no way to share
that information with anyone..
Imagine
if we had no way to exchange
or interact with our family or friends
Imagine
Not being able to use our facial expressions,
hands or body to gesture!?
Or mouth to speak!?
can you imagine?!?
We would have no way of sharing any information.
Picturing this should give us an appreciation
of the importance of this exchange.

As a story goes
When asked a older woman
How come she has so many friends
You see where I'm getting at
Unless we
empathically
effectively
peacefully
respectfully
successfully
and positively
make this exchange in communicating
There will be no point in living.

Body Language
66

I see you speaking to me
in more ways than one.
without having to open your mouth.
you don't have to open your mouth.
who says you have to open your mouth?
What you say,
conveys more or less than seven percent (7%)
of how you communicate.
Your tone, around thirty percent (30%)
Facial expressions, even more.
If you are observant,
you can tell if someone's interest
is consistent in what they are saying,
if he or she leans towards you while you are speaking as
oppose to having his or her arms folded
(which shows a lack of interest.)
or taking in context with the environment,
use common sense 'cause
possibly there aren't any armrests,
or it's presently cold..
WE DON'T KNOW!
But it does show
This is all in the way in which
our bodies speaks in a language,
foreign or domestic, cultural assimilated
Westernized as oppose to Middle Eastern.
It's not just what we say, it's how we say it
and how we look and act when we are saying it
so with that being said..

Before the English mistranslation
The justification of Adam and Eve living naked,
Before the game of charades,
Before sound was incorporated into film,
The public relied on actors and actresses

to portray their feelings
through facial expressions and body language

One of the first acts by captors
of their captives was to stripped them of their clothes
thereby reducing them to shame and humiliation.

How contriving
we are attracting members of the opposite sex
the same method applies
when we voluntarily choose to dress in a way
to turn heads by captivating someone's eye

The double standard of the sexes
When a man comments on a woman's dress,
he is considered misogynistic, sexist
but a woman dressing provocative,
she's somehow liberated and confident.

What's indirectly spoken by the members of our bodies
can either welcome or discourage a process
by which information is exchanged between individuals.
Keyword: exchange
because that information must be given and received
for communication to occur.
the mouth words one thing
eyes imply another
Facial features are misquoted
Misinterpreted in the perceiver's mind
as an opening. A pretext.
A smirk. A challenge
To pry the no thank you.
Cut scene to what's giving.
Given from the giver's form
Created a gesture storm walking away.

Moments where an innocent face to face impersonation
can quickly escalate to shifted shoulder about-face
Since nosey legs and hips butted into the conversation
the body suddenly shape clothes to formulate the initial say.
Comments colonize comfortability
Make conversing controversial cultural engineering.
See how easily the exchange can change the information
to where we are disrespecting each other unconsciously?

Back-masking what is heard
Your mind was telling them Nooo!
but your BODY!
Your BODY
Telling them Yeeesss!

Subliminally passed down,
downed lines of communication
for generations
Now this generation faced
with society's views of beauty and attraction.
finding themselves constantly
protracting (measuring up to)
what is considered sexy and appealing.
Abstraction of sight
Distraction from purpose
Extracting time
Detracting worth of self worth
for someone's hopes in unwrapping in time
gifted with that body and mind
The body will follow behind
or lead with tracks
Where the heart is deceived
without consulting the mind
retraction is blind.
Objectify.

Turning what's authentic to artificial to artifactual.
An increased association with body dissatisfaction
Attraction with eyes.
Attempting to get in to fit in
when the gap isn't wide
and when you're not verbally asking
to be sexually assaulted,
then you're attacked from the blind
the attacker with the same
orbitofrontal cortex
being misled, taught by the same society, about sex
and self control less,
influencing them, that's it ok to disrespect.
Therefore
dress in a way to decrease vulnerability,
take precautions of prevention
not everyone knows to practice self-control.

I'll leave you on this note.
During a time period in history,
where people lived in quiet kept communities
and kept their business to themselves
And if any outsider came speaking a different doctrine
They were tarred and feathered
sent way up stream
Where there were no roaming minutes
Because the message was sent!
Then times began changing.
effective leaders stop speaking up.
words and facial expressed conflict
in disagreement and the message
from the beginning was mixed.
it became confusion
and reading was easily misunderstood
Because no one could understand

what was said because
words were valued at seven percent (7%)
people no longer lived by what they preached.
So its important to be aware
of the messages we are sending
with our bodies.
What's the point of having our phones
and social media accounts on private
If we are not careful of the settings
we set in digital stone.
It's says a lot about our inner dialogue
Where every action
thought
and decision
is derived.

LESSONS

"What is done cannot be undone, but at least one can keep it from happening again."

Anne Frank

NO NEGATIVE THOUGHTS ALLOWED

Whatever negative thoughts you're having,
Throw them out the window
Yes!
Unscrew The Top Of Your Skull
Dig Inside Your Cerebral Cortex
Search Through Each Lobe,
Stop-nerve-signals-if-you-have-to!!
and pick out the negatives —
that's affecting your ability
and leading to your impulsive actions
Take them out now!
Before you listen any further
Take them out,
NOW!
I'll wait.
Are They Out Now?
Ok. Now think about what all you have,
be th-ank-ful..
Nah! Nah!
I said **No Negative Thoughts Allowed**
when thinking about what blessings
you have before you in the form
of family or friends
because they can be gone like snap!
Taken from you in any consequential detail fashion
that you didn't see coming
but you were warned about by parents!
Instead you were only focused on **those thoughts**
That led to every place besides home,
Those thoughts
That triggered every unpleasant body movement.
Those thoughts

<u>that's holding you back</u>
<u>from the best person **You Know You Can Be!**</u>
Be careful not to find fault with **those thoughts.**
Because you can pick out the negatives,
only later to discover they were the positives.
Instead of negating a gate around your mind
fencing the negatives out,
you housed them in.
As if you were your own audience
Booing yourself off stage.
it isn't your job to misjudge yourself.
But to overcome and endure through any hardship
you are cruising on at this time.
Let the CarGO that weighting you down
And again,
<u>think about the blessings you have</u>
<u>right in front you.</u>

NO ONE WINS

Against spoken language ravaging violently across seas
over seed's heads
at a close distance a close relation ship between loved ones,
No one wins,
When there are two speakers and half the listening.
No one wins,
In defense of their offenses.
No one wins,
When responding to disrespect with disrespect.
No one wins,
hiding behind insecure walls,
in justification of a conscious choice of being angry,
enraged.
No one wins,
When unearthing another's past skeletons.
Vocally exhibiting their museum of embarrassing moments
and poor choices in front of innocent onlookers
No one wins
Especially when it's the children doing the further
excavation, nothing humor bone about it.
No one wins
When hatred is layered in the heart
The inability to let go and love self
as we are to love each other.
No one wins
These inward battles never to be expressed outwards,
rewriting the history we forgotten we share occasionally.
No one wins
When there is no inner peace of being able to accept each
other.
No one wins!
No One Wins!
NO ONE WINS!
So why not suffer the loss.

Self-Respect, Stand On It

watch your

INTERNAL and

EXTERNAL Language

It Is **SOUL** *Dangerous*!

Make sho there's no barriers

And they're both speaking the same thing

or else its b?ᵃ?b?bᵃl?i?n?g?

What you think to yourself
And about yourself
plays a major role
In whether or not you **RESPECT** yourself.

because there will already be
EXTERNAL forces

to chip away at your **SELF WORTH**

without you contributing to them.
So don't b o m b a r d yourself
with ̶n̶e̶g̶a̶t̶i̶v̶e̶ self-talk.

psssss you are helping
in the devaluing process.

The ground which you stand
have this gravitational pull,
that will determine your standard.
Do you cheat? That's Your Standard.
Lie? That's Your Standard.
Steal? That's your Standard.
or are you striving to be honest
and fair with self and others?

76

STAND on something
worth **STANDING** for!

Continue to tell yourself
words that will build you up!
Whether we realize this or not
our minds have this tendency
to believe everything we tell it.

So will the next šĭť ďŏwň or walk self-talk
leave you vulnerable to the influences
that lead to indulging in vomiting behavior
that will subtlety affect your mental physical,
emotional and spiritual health?
That is something you should ask yourself.

That's why it's **SOUL** important to watch
your I N T E R N A L language
and how you speak your self worth.

By setting our standards on moral HIGH
we won't settle for anything less,
to **(fit)(in)** or feel negatively accepted
when we will have already accepted ourselves.

Self Respect. Stand On It.

BLIND BEAUTY

[Indistinct chatter] in my ear canal tells of true beauty.
How you, lower your tone controlled,
Compose compound your sound.
You are spoken choice words,
Chewed on before spat out.
Parental done right.

I hear heart-beating drum; ear balancing being,
you being all imagined without sight but sound.
sincere. synchronized with self.
So so sound.
solid. secure. sane through noise.
going back through noise poised.
I see you ain't ever scared **aye**!
You ain't ever scared **aye**!
I hear-feel you.
I see-Braille you.
beauty beneath the complexity of your skin.
your complexion doesn't compare justice
to your content's crown.
your character be royalty through tried consistency,
just keep going.

Nothing is made beautiful
without dark, pressure, heat-tested and trial.
though it's a process,
Just keep wrinkling facial muscle exposing cheeks,
dimples, teeth and smile.
It's for your internal benefit.
Containing your craziness.
From your own worst criticism.
For the beholder beholding your beauty
are for moments forevermore.

Blind Beauty is a lifestyle.
Blind Beauty has been your life now.
As you see through specs
correcting vision for a clearer path
to walk on in this hate filled world.

So you be bifocal point.
You be so many things to say,
but I'll sticky reminder you on this note..
your benevolent, altruism, affable vibrates the sound
so when you speak on your beauty's behalf,
you do so impartial.

All this to say,
I'm literally a simp for an intelligent woman
with glasses.
You Blind Beauty You.

Love Without Seeing

I don't even know you and I love you.
Similar to the experience of
when a woman comes to know
the joyful news that she is pregnant.
and from that moment of conception
she begins making changes in her lifestyle.
In order to ensure the safety and health of her unborn child.
For example,
she watches her eating habits
Cuts off unnecessary risks like drugs and alcohol.
She prepares. Educates herself.
And she never seen this child except by ultrasound,
She loves, deeply, It's profound!
Lost in others.
Putting all her heart, soul, and might
into this child she doesn't expect to see.
Until nine months are up
and the baby is conceived.
When conceived, the baby clings dear life to mother.
And it takes a while for the new born as well to see that
person who loved them enough to ensure they were born
healthy and could breathe.
And the child smiles when his or her eyes finally opens up.
This is part of what love does without seeing.
Like children playing without racism
Taught peace without hatred
The love on their faces for the other child
they "SEE" without discriminating
Is the exact way how I feel about you.
Amazing how this deep care of concern and consideration
can do to the innermost.
Unselfish when love is giving in control fashion.
The willingness and steadfastness
in making similar changes to be that righteous example.

Daily self-examination,
cleansing this past dirt off my face.
Applying this Peaceful Solution
Character Education to show you.
You don't need sight to love
Through actions is how I love you.
Peace.

Love Do Know Boundaries

How foolish, unconditional my heart was. Sometimes is.
Allowing any and everything in without filter.
Not great to keep the lifeblood pace flowing.

At an early age it wasn't a focal curriculum to build
internal fences, just don't burn bridges.
Not everyone is privileged
to enter your home without conditions.
Though unconditionally without restrictions,
I was told to love limitlessly,
Is how I allowed in the ideal of what we called love,
and was conditioned.

Spousal abuse shampoo wash
my definition of what I thought was true love.
With soap in eyes, no matter each other's problems
We was to accept without correction.

Love, I thought was patient, kind and endures all things,
was I right?
had me questioning, why are loved ones,
the ones we relearn love from?
Without a biological,
I had to seek My Spiritual Father for help
to know what love is and what love is not
showing love too has limits.

For how can heal and hurt equate love?
Only makes sense if it is to make change.
That's how I was conditioned to believe love was
unconditional.

That no matter what the other person does or did,

I was to love without limiting their behavior towards me.
And not limit their behavior towards me.
Enabling the effects of their behavior towards everyone.
Perceiving this to be true love.

But how can love protect and abuse in intermediate
intervals of years?
If love is to be transmitted out must it first be within?
So why isn't the beholder who is supposed to have love
within not giving it out?
Was it something I missed?
Is it not within their limits to express?
This cannot be love!
So you meaning to tell me,
love doesn't have self control?
If the one exhibiting love in love
when they act out of love!?

Because they are about to make me lose my mind,
Up In Here! Up In Here!
if they hit me one mo' 'gain out of their love.
Oh! let me guess, it's only love being it's "unrestricted",
"no limit", "boundary-less", "unconditional" self again.
How can I accept this, without the feeling of guilt or fear?

This is what occurs when we teach about love
and not teach that it needs to be guarded like the heart.
See the human heart has a wall
that is approximately five inches long,
3.5 inches wide, 2.5 inches thick,
roughly the size of your fist.
With male's heart weighing in the heaviest.
I read this metaphorically as sign
of sadness, sorrow and disease.
So not only is the world baring stress on man's shoulder.

It's affecting his ability to spread pure love to his members.
Which he leans on the heart of his counterpart
which weighs the less
but definitely not the least, for support.
This, is why we must guard wholeheartedly Love.

Even if the threats are inside.
The heart has a way to oxygenate deoxygenated blood.
For the guardians of true love have one job.
Call me the President
Ready to shutdown this government to secure love.

To the immigrants who invaded my skin,
The ones I share intimate aspects of me
and expanded my kingdom with.
No one is exempt from the One Torah
given to the naive and the stranger.

Out of ignorance,
I unconditionally loved you enough
that it brought the nation danger.
When I kept allowing you back in the gates.
Interrupting the natural law of cause and effect,
reaping what you sow.
Taking the hit for you when it's meant for you
to undergo pain, so that you will learn and change.
The best I did for you,
separating myself was love for you.
No longer rescuing you from your irresponsibility.
Foolish to have thought I could make the right choice for
you, consequently I was not helping you.

Something we all need to learn,
love isn't a game to be played.
Don't save them, if they do not want to be saved.

I understand that now.
Because love does the same.

When we speak love
we speak it's boundaries into existence.
In effect showing what love is and what it isn't.
a.k.a it's limits.
Love and hate can't coexist.
We are not being unloving
when we are forced to protect love
from those who seek to kill it.

I wouldn't love you if I didn't want to see you change.
Because my love for you is to see you on your own make
positive self-change.

I'm only telling you what I learn from Abba Yahweh
and experience.
Guard your heart mind with all diligence
for out of it flows the springs of life.

Love do know boundaries.

MY IDEAL OF HER

My ideal of her is a picture. perfect. blur.

See I'm a over-thinker.
so I over think her until her
abstract mural is made vivid
on concrete thought;
meaning,
I can see her now.
But then, I'm back to photo
editing.
Constantly brightening
contrast images.
comparing blends
between screen,
I overlay layers.
now careful of who occupy
organ's opacity
It seems the more I open,
some tend through levels of
control
exploit my transparency.
I got the problem already detected see,
It's due to the settings I set.
So I crop around quality differences,
of what I like from this pic. dislike from that pic.
Now with a sharpened vision
from being picky as detail.
Not to fade out boundaries.
So this project won't project a vignette copy of the past.

So my ideal of her

is most definitely smart,
Because I'm a smart ass.
Coming from a former class clown.
She acts class
because she had a consistent mama
and dad figure in her life.
She wasn't broken.
A two parent home dynamic was important.
It's according to how she respects me right.
And how I love her right.
The healthy cycle.

Ah, I love how intelligent she is so
stereotypical hood.
and academically savvy, artsy, witty,
a covert comedian.
that type of humor when it's dark.
I'm falling asleep while driving.
she's the high beams, horn blazing
coming from the opposite end of road
I veered off to.
Forewarning and keeping me alert.
when I come to, it being all a dream.
in actuality waking up a victim to a water and flour prank.
Then I get mad.
She uncontrollably laughs.
She don't know she just started a prank war.
So I simultaneously begin to laugh with her.
but at her.
thinking of all the ways to get her back
and it's done in fun.

She shows me every day
how she's the one.
She never runs from problems,
she faces them head on,
courageously; meaning, despite fear.
She turns off that independent switch,
And we work cooperatively.
None of that competitive drift.
Embraces change and correction
with submissive arms of humility.

We both came as we are.
And becoming better as the days progress.
I like to Shoutout Mr. Reality
for speaking this into existence.
Because I think she's the one man.
Although I prefer her to be born
in the middle of the fourth and fifth Roman month
or any,
I ain't that picky.
except for a Gemini.
For me, we vibe compatibly not just chemistry.
YAHmazing how this came into fruition.

She's gift wrapped modestly .
easy to unwrap moderately.
taking my time this time honestly.
Rushing the package can damage the product.
And I'm a patient patient.
And she so opposite end of the table.
the polar opposite of me.
we magnetically attract.
siamese attach-ment to be joined at the chest,
my heart mate.
for we sharpen each other's perspectives.

extract contents from our continents
to strengthen each of our characters.

Like The Messiah do not called men.
It's the spirit of My Father that draws them.
specifically her.
for what Yahweh brought together, let no man,
including our inner man or woman tear apart.
Yea I want that 613 bond.
That "I'll love you when your hair turns grey and I'll still
want you if you gain a little weight" bond.

I never want her to be and she's not Eve-perfect .
Because I'm not Adam-perfect.
See what hurt Adam and Eve's perfect,
Is all they knew was perfect.
And not the imperfect process it took to get there.
See she's familiar with the struggle
and what it took to get here.
She knows the grind the bustle of survival.
the wickedness of idle
and being worshipped as a idol.
She Yahweh all day everyday!
Our purpose never repurposed.
we know our role's worth.
And the contribution to make roles work.
we be sunrise full moon working side by side.
when the sun rays ricochet from the shades,
hitting both of our eyes in the morning time.
Not ashamed of our nakedness
for we enter this sinful world having nothing
and being open with nothing to hide.
I'm the head and she's gladly the body
which encompasses the spine.
The glue that holds the family together.

I get jealous sometimes,
by her healthy eating habits
for she don't mind healthy
for her heart soul and mind healthy
You know she cooking mine healthy
a healthy body will follow a mind healthy
because it's already too much mental illness to deal with,
making our journey more stress free.
She doesn't get caught up in the hype
She knows dem scriptures and her history.

A Sweettart with a Sweetheart.
The crazy I can handle.
An unstable creature at times.
Reminds me of Sweetpea's line
from The Movie Baby Boy.
When I was a baby boy.
I thought and spoke as a baby boy.
Every day becoming a better man.
And putting away toddler tendencies
That's why I can handle her crazy with leniency.

She's
my walking prayer.
A prayer I prayed with my feet,
Meaning when she was somewhere working on her,
I was in another place working on me.
But who am I kidding! Hahaha!!
THIS WOMAN DOESN'T EXIST! Hahaha

And it be right when I least expected
One day I was walking,
stumbled over my stubbornness,
someone quickly came to assist.
I lifted my head slightly.
And there..
Quoting Scripture
"a righteous man's steps are ordered by Yahweh ..
though he stumble,
he will not be utterly cast down by Yahweh,
for righteous Yahweh holds him up with His hands."
And in my head I replied: there you are.
You exist.

DEAR MASCULINITY

Word on the street is "you too much to carry." **You** "contraband, arms, no hugs to bury". **You** "insensitive". **You** a "dawg"! **They** sense sniff your scent but can't seem to sense your fear. **You** "emotionless". **They** talk like we don't need your protection. **Like** you don't provide traffic lights, street signs you erect on every corner. **They** tryna stop your yields to oncoming. **Like** your legend don't impact map for visual direction. **Since** they ain't helping in the construction. **All** they see from you is destruction.

Society really got a hit out on you. **Those** hits are not love taps, **rather** clandestine acts turn stats. **Critical** licks. **Pettiness**. **Catching** up for all the birthdays they purposefully missed. **When** you birth by genetics, man. **Ironic**, the most among the **parentless** homes **homeless**, **youth** runaways, **behavioral** issues, **the** war slain, **depressed**, **suicide**, **incarcerated**. **And** they haven't realize yet, an attack on you is really an attack on our female counterpart. **There** are things a man can do, a woman cannot, **vice-versa**.

It's obvious they're not looking to understand your physiology. **Hooked** only on your physicality. **This** new age quick to label you toxic. **SJWs** tryna silent Jay's Ws'. **Would** get Mike-check'd **tryna** make lite of your Magic. **How** you pulled Bird from hot flashes. **A** bad boy before the Bad Boys. **They** forget how you Glide through Barkley **Sent** the Sonics' waves. **Packed** up the Hoya Destroya. **Penny** couldn't afford a dime. **Out** Miller'd every time. **You** was COVID delivering The Mailman his Stockton's. **It's** a team's dream to go **Six** times! **Six** times! **Six** times! **Six** times! **Six** times! **Six** times! **yo** last dance never cakewalk! **Your** competitive nature turnt ya boy into a man.

In actuality, you really showed how when competing
against self can turn a boy into a man.
Part of me believe they know it and it's planned.
I'm convinced the *American Psychological Association*
is run by a bunch of misandrists; haters of men. **How** they
confuse traditional with toxicity. **Aggression** with drive.
Dominance, with competent leadership, **Self-leading**
becoming one of the greatest of all time. **And** they hate
how you make fathers present. **This** is for the mass-to-cue-
lens-to-see. **Masculinity** isn't just to mask tears to memes.
And you didn't mask your tears when your father died,
Instead you harness those emotions deep inside and made
every one better around you.

I use Micheal Jeffery Jordan's career as an analogy to show
you, **how** you are a franchise. **Without** you, **I'll** be a
summer league player competing for a roster spot.

As you transat through translation. **version** after version.
Through Protest. **Attempts** to rewrite, rewired what's
handwritten in ribonucleic history. **Forever** in your DNA
permeating through man's makeup. **This** my way to
makeup, **through** writing you. **To** never rewrite to rewire
you, **into** a ticking time bomb to expired you. **I'm** writing
because **I** never knew how much of you was wired in me.
This envied, the enemy wanted my temple empty
of your innate energy **I** renege quickly. **I** knew your effect
wasn't a defect to eject when I became resistant. **A** stoic
stone; **hardened** after a confrontation. **Conscious** of your
closeness.
I'm learning to accept flaws and all. **Get** up and grow with
every fall. **Masculinity**, you make me strong.
Although articles artificial you to try to make you into
something artifactual.

It's ok to be a man. **Boys** will be boys **because** they are
born boys with the same masculine energy
My stance is where are the real masculine man who do not
deny them? **Or** deprive them with guidance?
Or get crossed up in the crosshair of crossfires?
Or become News Headliners or highlighters of violence?
To make life hard to provide them.

Our young males, need a man there **to** reflect **to** direct
eye-to-eye, facial, body contact **to** clinch hand
Return to **re-step** to **re-read**
The basic instruction before leaving earth.
To *"train up a child in His way that they should go,*
and as they grow they will not depart from it".

Re-educating me how you are not toxic.
It is a lack of you to why we grow into men unconscious,
despondent, reprehensible and irresponsible with power.
The problem is too much emphasis of caricature and not on
the development of moral character.
Because weak men enable wicked men to do wickedly.
Real men take a real stand to tap into integrity.
Real men man up! **Yea** real man make mistakes,
But real man own up! **Real men** don't abuse! **Real men**
don't rape! **Real men** take you and lay down their life for
the safety of their family and making our world into a
better place. **I** just had enough of listening to some poets
emasculate you.

So I thank Him for you and you for making any man into a
better man.

Sincerely,
A better man.

94

Be Kind To EveryOne You Meet

for you do not know what battle
What war-torn house
divided against themselves.
What pressure. What inferno.
What foot underneath.
What hard place, Mac-truck in between.
What love, what hate, what mixture,
What second, what minute, what hour,
What day it has been.
What voice, what help,
what counsel they have received.
And your words
could be the needle that sows love
or the hand glove they lose grip of,
from the cliff, that they were hoping
it could had saved them from.

Smile

If you are wondering why I'm smiling.
It is because I see you.
Like the flu it spreads.
fed by the thoughts led feeling
into camera. I'm all satisfied action. Lights.
Shining example through cheek's muscles.
A Viral reminder to lift up self when down.
Who got time for a frown
when you can release endorphins.
It's not easy to mask, through stress
but it's worth endorsing.
Strengthen immune systems worldwide
by this contagion; smile.
Sterilizing those pains and struggles.
noticed we are more approachable,
people rather engage on a social level.
When wearing a horizontal parentheses
You become are more leveled.
If forcing ourselves to smile
to think pass the past
so do it.
Now I encourage you
Go and bring joy
to others.